sister sister sister sister sister sister sister sister siste
sister sister sister sister sister sister sister sister sister
er sister sister sister sister sister sister sister sister siste
sister sister s   ster sister sister sister
er sister siste   sister sister sister siste
sister sister   ter sister sister sister
er sister sister   sister sister sister siste
sister sister sister sister sister sister sister sister sister
er sister sister sister sister sister sister sister sister siste
sister sister sister sister sister sister sister sister sister
er sister sister sister sister sister sister sister sister siste
sister sister sister sister sister sister sister sister sister
er sister sister sister sister sister sister sister sister siste
sister sister sister sister sister sister sister sister sister
er sister sister sister sister sister sister sister sister siste
sister sister sister sister sister sister sister sister sister
er sister sister sister sister sister sister sister sister siste
sister sister sister sister sister sister sister sister sister
er sister sister sister sister sister sister sister sister siste
sister sister sister sister sister sister sister sister sister
er sister sister sister sister sister sister sister sister siste

Assalāmu' Alaykum

B.U.K.S™ has been inspired by the significance that Islām places on knowledge, kinship and mutual love. Inshā'Allāh, we hope the books in this series will:

– Inform and inspire the reader through relevant Āyā and Sahīh Hadīth
– Express many of the emotions that you may wish to convey. At times we have all been lost for words, unable to say what we really feel.

We pray Inshā'Allāh, that these books provide a treasured gift and hence unite your kindred spirits, so that you can truly say;

"I love you" not only as a means of personal expression, but also that;

"I love you for the sake of Allāh." (Abu Dāwūd)

BUKS™
Books.Unite.Kindred.Spirits

A gift for

_____

from

_____

SISTER

an Islamic Perspective

Published by:
Siratt Group
PO Box 8141,
Nottingham,
NG2 7XS, UK
Email: info@siratt.com
Website: www.siratt.com

Product No:
ISBN 1-90 5258-04-06

For Sales
Order online – on our Internet site at www.siratt.com. We have partnered with worldpay.com to provide our online credit card payment solution. This specialist company provides the highest levels of security available in transmitting and processing credit card transactions.

Please note:

Whenever Allāh's name or the Prophet is mentioned within this book, it is good practise to recite:

Allāh (swt) - Subḥānahu wa taʻāla – Glorified be Allāh, the Most High

Prophet (saw) - ṢallAllāhu ʻalayhi wasallam – May the peace and blessings of Allāh be upon him

[Sūrah number:verse] - Qur'ānic quote followed by reference in square brackets

(Bukhārī) - Saḥīh Hadīth or other source followed by reference in curved brackets.

He who likes that his sustenance should be expanded and his age may be lengthened should join the tie of kinship.

(Muslim)

Māshā'Allāh a sister's love is one of a kind
She'll offer gifts, favours and plenty of time
A sister's love is manifested in so many ways
From adult years right back to childhood days
From harsh truths to an encouraging word
Hers' is the voice that I long to be heard.

And hold fast, all of you together to the
rope of Allāh, and do not separate…

[Q:103]

Recounting each childhood pleasure
And sorrow in varying measure
A special theme links the two:
Al-Ḥamdulillāh I shared them with you.

Al-Wāsil is not the one who recompenses the good done to him by his relatives, but Al-Wāsil is the one who keeps good relations with those relatives who had severed the bond of kinship with him.

(Bukhārī)

I remember so much about you;
Your generosity when times were hard,
Protecting me, always being my guard.
I remember the stories we would tell,
At night, about Heaven and Hell.
How we'd have our midnight treats,
By sneaking up chocolates and sweets,
How Abu would tell us to be quiet,
To stop jumping and making a riot.
How we would pretend to be asleep,
Yet under the covers with giggles we'd weep.
You were the one on whom I could depend,
Not only a sibling but also my 'best friend'.
My dear sister things are still the same,
And I pray Inshā'Allāh they never change.

Sisterhood is a loving relationship
Where naught is desired in return
Save strengthening the ties of kinship
For which the hearts do yearn.

Messenger of Allāh said: Eat together and be not separate,
because blessing is only with the united body.

(Ibn Mājah)

I remember crying when we were told we wouldn't always be together
How so? When Inshā'Allāh our hearts are connected for now and forever.

And the believers, men and women, are protecting
friends of one another; they enjoin the right and
forbid the wrong...

[Q9:71]

Let no person, thing or worldly temptation,
Raise us above our station.
Let us value our bond of kinship,
By treasuring our special relationship.
My dear sister, Al-Ḥamdulillāh , we share so much
Our childhood, parents, memories and dīn
After this our temporary journey
Inshā'Allāh I pray we share the treasures of the Unseen.

Sisterhood is knowing that someone else's
heart is aching along with yours.

Nurse no grudge, nurse no aversion and do not
sever ties of kinship and live like fellow-brothers
as servants of Allāh.

(Muslim)

Warmth radiates from you to all you meet.
'Assalāmu 'Alaykum' you say as you take your seat.
Never waiting for others to mend broken ties
You ignore all the slander, the gossip and the lies.
You nurse no grudge, you nurse no aversion
May Allah bless your strong determination.

You were always there to help me,
'Encouraging' when others were disparaging.
You directed me to the way of Islam,
And to never do anyone harm.
How precious was this bond of kinship,
With Islam the heart of this relationship.
A sister is - a 'blood-bond' of destiny;
A test, like all others, to determine our sincerity.
And even though we had our fights
Our loyalty always remained so tight
Every day I thank Allāh for blessing me,
Inshā'Allāh I pray our love lasts eternally.

Messenger of Allāh said, "You shall not enter Paradise till you believe; and you will not believe till you love one another. Shall I not guide you to a thing? When you will do it, you will love one another. Spread peace among you."

(Muslim)

Charity given to a poor person is charity and charity given to a relative earns two rewards: one for giving charity and one for upholding the ties of kinship.

(Tirmidhī)

I remember the days when you'd take the blame
No one else would have done the same.
You have always been there to see me right;
Without pride, arrogance or spite.
On you I have come to depend,
As my mentor, sister and friend.
I just wanted to tell you before it's too late,
That you are truly my loyal soul mate.

As believers our greatest consolation when our loved ones depart is the divine promise of eternal reconciliation for those of us whom Allāh blesses.

Subḥān Allāh you are my perspective on the past.

You will see the believers in their mutual kindness, love and sympathy just like one body. When a limb complains, the whole body responds to it with wakefulness and fever.

(Bukhārī and Muslim)

I wish for you all the best,
Your dreams, du'ās and the rest.
Without doubt your secrets I shall never tell,
Inshā'Allāh I pray in Paradise we both shall dwell.

JazākAllāh khair for reminding me
With absolute conviction and sincerity
That wordly worries are only temporary
And to Allāh we shall return eternally.

My dear beloved sister
Whether it was putting up with my mood
Or buying me gifts and take-away food
Or teaching me the correct supplication
I do say with everlasting justification
Through every discussion and counsel with you
My sweet sister you have always managed to
Administer some comfort to my heart
Whether close at hand or far apart
Your love overcomes distance and reaches me
With absolute warmth and sincerity.

The person who severs the bond of kinship will not enter Paradise.

(Bukhārī)

Al-Ḥamdulillāh, you feature within so many of my memories.
It seems strange to recall…something which has no mention of you.

And there may spring from you a nation who invite to goodness, and enjoin right conduct and forbid indecency. Such are they who are successful.

[Q3:104]

I truly thank Allāh for blessing me with you:
Friend, mentor, teacher and sister too
Māshā'Allāh! How many roles you have played
Inshā'Allāh by you I shall never be betrayed.

You're the first person I want to share
News with-good or bad
Someone to share my joy with
Or console me when I'm sad
The simple pleasures in life are magnified
Greatly when I share them with you
Shared laughter and tears, hopes and fears
Invoking Allāh to bless us forever
Praying that we'd always stay together
But Inshā'Allāh whatever Allāh deems best
For this Life and the next
Whether we are near or far apart
You will always be here in my heart.

Other Siratt Giftbook titles include:

WIFE
an Islamic Perspective
ISBN 1-905258-00-3

HUSBAND
an Islamic Perspective
ISBN 1-905258-01-1

MOTHER
an Islamic Perspective
ISBN 1-905258-02-X

FATHER
an Islamic Perspective
ISBN 1-905258-03-8

SISTER
an Islamic Perspective
ISBN 1-905258-04-6

BROTHER
an Islamic Perspective
ISBN 1-905258-05-4

FRIEND
an Islamic Perspective
ISBN 1-905258-06-2

SIRATT®
designed to remind

Siratts' range comprises a number of high quality Islamic products these include:

The much sought after Islamic LifeBook
Gregorian and Islamic diaries
Beautifully illustrated Islamic calendars
All occasion greeting cards
Original Islamic artwork prints, Islamic Telephone Directory,
Islamic Baby Journal, Islamic Wedding Planner
And
A selection of Islamic gift books.

For further information and online purchases please visit
www.siratt.com